# BALANCE SHEETS

# BALANCE SHEETS

A
Collection
Of
Poems

MARK SCOTT

KU
PRESS

A CIP catalogue record for this book is available from the British Library

ISBN 9781909362598

Typeset in Baskerville

Editorial and Design by Kingston University MA Publishing Students: Courtney E Thompson, Fiona R Paterson, Maria C Nae, Nathan M Dann and Shada Elmansouri

First published in Great Britain 2022 Kingston University Press Kingston University Penrhyn Road, Kingston-upon-Thames KT1 2EE

For Jeff Aeling, Kevin Ducey, Jeff Hess,
John Martin, Amy Metier, and Amy Lemon Olson

In Memoriam: Reg Saner

# CONTENTS

# III.

# IV.

# V.

# VI.

# VII.

## VIII.

Acknowledgments
About the Author
About Kingston University Press

# FOREWORD

## I. On Transcendence

After an interview for a teaching position at St. John's College (Santa Fe) in 2005, I was asked to explain what I meant—"just a few lines of additional comment might help us to get to know you better as a thinker"— when I said "there is no transcendence." I answered: I meant, "I don't see anything beyond life and death." I remember thinking, even before I said the word "transcendence," that I was in trouble, that it wasn't the word I wanted, that it wasn't the syntax I wanted, that it wasn't the topic (religious belief, faith, etc.) I wanted.

Emerson once noted that a neighbor of his defined "transcendental" as meaning "a little beyond." I think that almost every thing, word, and idea comes fringed or hazed with other things, words, and ideas. Literature, and poetry in particular, records this phenomenon— and continually fails to put a stop to it. There's always a last word a little beyond the most recent last word. As I write this, it occurs to me that the scientific method, too, allows for something that escapes the present horizon of experiment, the evidence or hint for which is presently within that horizon.

You ask me if there is "a poetic or literary sense of transcendence." I think so. And metaphor, or "translation," as Bacon calls it in the *Advancement*, is a useful exemplar of it. As Derrida points out in "White Mythology," metaphor is a little beyond Aristotle's system of poetics: Aristotle himself says so. Derrida stipulates that Aristotle marginalizes what he can't center; I would say that Derrida can't quite center what Aristotle can't quite marginalize. Thinkers before Aristotle could neither marginalize nor have the last word on metaphor; that Derrida couldn't do the latter 2,300 years later

i

isn't surprising. Metaphor, as Levi-Strauss might say, is *bon à penser*—good to think; but it can't be thought *through* or worked *out*.

I don't think metaphor is the only thing that's a little beyond our capacity to wrap up or keep under wraps. In one of his songs, Paul Simon says, "Everybody loves the sound of the train in the distance; everybody thinks it's true." In a later verse, he glosses his metaphor: the sound of the train in the distance is "the thought that life could be better"—a thought, he says, that seems "woven indelibly into our heart and our brain." William James said so repeatedly. May one say that this thought of transcendence itself can't be transcended? Faulkner in his Nobel Prize speech said as much.

And this, to skip a lot of exposition, is why I think literature matters: it records our limitations and our constant desire to be done with them, both of which suffer again in translation and provoke correction. When I read the canonical authors, I, like Machiavelli, "trasferisco in loro," beyond my limitations, beyond these limits of time and place (but not much, and not for long), into theirs and those.

## II. Libra

In 1995, knowing that I was about to be unemployed, a friend paid for me to use the services of Alumnae Resources, a job search and counseling organization in San Francisco. My counselor had me take a small battery of tests, among which the Myers-Briggs Type Indicator stood out because it reminded me of the examination Warren Beatty undergoes on applying to the Parallax Corporation. I rented *The Parallax View* that night. I had nothing better to do. While waiting for the results, I was given another test, the SkillScan. It asks you to list those skills for which you had minimal or no ability. There I excelled: "prepare food, manage records, repair/restore, build/construct, calculate/compute, budget, facilitate groups, create images, take care of others, negotiate, sell." I was then asked to check off, on a list of "Functional/Transferable Skills," twenty skills I used in the job I no longer had, and to circle ten that I "preferred" to use. I circled *read, compare, edit, analyze, synthesize, integrate, write, improvise, counsel, listen,* and *public speaking.*

The third test was called the Strong Interest Inventory. According to the Summary, I had a "very high interest" in nothing that fell under the categories of creating or enjoying art, selling or managing, helping or instructing, accounting or processing data, building or repairing, researching or analyzing. My interests in art, writing, athletics, music/dramatics, and merchandising were "average."

Two dots in the gray area between Dissimilar and Similar, the "Mid-Range," indicated that I had very dissimilar or merely dissimilar interests from all but two of the forty occupations listed under the categories "Realistic" and "Investigative." Tracing over to the left, I saw that I was, in effect, indifferent about being a College Professor or a Psychologist. Under the Artistic and Social Occupations, I fared better. My highest scores came under the Artistic Occupations. The highest of the high? Advertising Executive. The lowest? Medical Illustrator.

If I wanted to settle on indifference as a career path, my choices were numerous: Hair Stylist, Human Resources Director, Investments Manager, Life Insurance Agent, Realtor, Travel Agent, and Business Education Teacher. In the end, the Strong Interest Inventory measured style: "Personal Style," "Work Style," "Learning Environment Style," "Leadership Style," and "Risk

Taking/Adventure Style." True to my sign, Libra, I hung in the balance. I preferred to work alone; I preferred to work with people. I preferred a practical working environment; I preferred an academic environment. I wasn't comfortable taking charge of others; I was comfortable taking charge of others. I disliked adventure and risk taking; I liked adventure and risk taking.

On Tax Day, the results of the Myers-Briggs Type Indicator were returned to my counselor. With one exception, I showed no "clear preference" for "extraversion" over "introversion," for "intuition" over "sensing," for "thinking" over "feeling." Out of a possible score of 60, I registered a 37 for "perceiving" over "judging." "There are sixteen possible types," my counselor told me. "You're an ENTP." She flipped the Report Form over to let me read the "characteristics frequently associated" with the ENTP "type":

> Quick, ingenious, good at many things. Stimulating company, alert and outspoken. May argue for fun on either side of a question. Resourceful in solving new and challenging problems, but may neglect routine assignments. Apt to turn to one new interest after another. Skillful in finding logical reasons for what they want.

I took exception to being ingenious, resourceful, and logical, but the rest was accurate enough. What helped most in the month or two I spent with Alumnae Resources was being reminded how many occupations there were, if I had ever known how many. None of this testing or counseling helped me to get my next job, which came down to a choice between cleaning houses for $7 an hour and smoking salmon for $8. I chose to smoke salmon.

## III. The Best Damned Poet in the Business

Poetry is the temporary lending of significance, most of which it borrows from history, for lack of a better creditor. But the books can never be balanced: this is Scott's Law. Which reminds me: "the chief business of the American people is business. They are profoundly concerned with producing, buying, selling, investing, and prospering in the world." So said Calvin Coolidge, the 30th President of the United States, in a speech he gave almost 100 years ago.

On the day I graduated from college in 1982, a fellow graduate, who for two years had been generous with her steady supply of cocaine, threw a party with her housemates. She told the five of us that her father would be there. We'd never met him, but we'd heard of him: he was "a shipping magnate." And then there he was, our Onassis, flown into Denver on his jet and chauffeured up to Boulder, for all we knew. The party had just started, but he was already looking at his watch. We couldn't come up with an unintelligible way to thank him for the funds his daughter had diverted to our cause. I decided to introduce myself. In no time, he had me backed up against the central column in the playroom. "So," he said, "what do you do?" Something possessed me—language, probably, which is always ready for anything—to tell him what I was. And this, according to notes I made at the time, and lost after typing them up, is what he said to that:

> Okay, you're a poet. You gotta have no ego. You can't have an ego. Worrying is worthless. You can't worry about the megaton bomb. It's useless. I couldn't be effective if I did. You have to be effective. Everyone in business is a climber. But you have to climb the right mountain, be a Hillary,

climb the Everests. If someone says no more three-drawer filing cabinets, you have to think, how about a two-drawer? Change is good. We accept change. You get an A. Today is your day to begin to become the best in the business. Tell them to go screw themselves. Stocks and bonds don't interest me. I know all the heads of the airlines. Braniff's wife decorated their planes and they went belly-up. The goal is infinity. Goal and change are of a different order. Change means new ways to maximize profit. It's a byproduct of the way to the goal itself. The mountain is not to sit on but to climb. You get an A. Money means nothing unless you do what makes you happy. But if you have this opportunity, and every uncommon person does, you have to work in your happiness until you're the best in the business— poetry, plumbing parts, or shipping, I don't care. As long as you're the best. The best damned poet in the business.

In some sense, all the poems in this book, even the few written before 1982, are embroiled answers to what Mr. Robinson said, and to what the United States said, and didn't say, through him. Only a few of them have that permanent scowl, my mother, that owl, predicted for my forehead from my adolescent fury, if I didn't run around the block instead of worry.

# I.

                    but as
Fishes glide, leaving no print where they passe,
Nor making sound; so closely thy course goe,
Let men dispute, whether thou breathe, or no.

—John Donne, "To Sir Henry Wotton" (1598)


How very pleasant it must be
For little fishes in the sea!
They never learn to swim at all,
It came to them when they were small.

—Alice Farwell Brown, "Fishes" (1908)

# Spiral

A football in a spiral is beautiful.
A lemon is, whole salmon are.
They used to spiral, avoiding
the human, on a farm
run by Norwegians in Chile.
Their eyes like their scales the least light take
and show off, more silent out of the water now
than in, if silence *(sauvage*, integral) have degrees.

Latching on behind an occipital,
I lift your cold thigh; my cup of coffee,
cooled off considerably, has scales
on the surface, of half and half;
I spill it toward my mouth,
bigger than a fish's and less efficient,
hoping surface tension
works to my advantage this time,
as the squamous side
clings to the surface of the bath, salt or fresh.

Sometimes we cut it closer to where
our medulla would be,
which keeps that football curve alive,
a hump, a powerful shoulder
still purposeful, kinetic, upstreaming to spawn—
or so in my salmon envy I like to think.
Smoked, they have a shelf-life of three weeks.

# How To Carry Salmon

I'll tell you how to carry salmon in a smokehouse.
Salmon from a farm are like city kids
to salmon that run wild. We're burdened with syntax.
The salmon talk, or would; I lift their heads on the faucet
and look at them still swim, if they could.

Their teeth are sharp, my oral exam;
depressing, their tongue's too thin and narrow for syntax.
But what a nose, what a throat, what shoulders
if they had them! I get no answer.

On the skin, coral and jet geometries;
in the book, talk of Deadwood,
a plant in a pickup-bed's smidgen of sand.
The salmon glom on to the gardening tubs,
adhere; no water gets underneath their skin—
they're insolvent.

S-V-O: that order of cognac and syntax—
such labels as I come across,
macerated salmon fragments down the drains
with paint chips off the floor—
repeated attempts to say the thing once more:
the salmon's shoulder,
driving up the farm's powerless corridors.

It's upstream, to get a clean utterance,
place enough, in the light-industrial sun.
We're burdened with syntax.
Light, *siccum* light.
On graduation day, put your robes on.

# At the Scandinavian Smokehouse

## (San Francisco)

"Salmon from Norway smells like butter lettuce,
but cucumbers smell like Norwegian salmon."
"Yes, that smell's the salmon," the boss said.
"But not the salmon from Chile," I said.
"Different farms, different kinds of salmon."
"Maybe the ice in Norway makes the difference."
"They pack it better there, much better,"
he said, and flicked cubes off the Styrofoam.
"The Chilean melted three days ago."

Days later, when they dropped off that salmon from the Sacramento,
a king, hook-jawed and humped from its deadening voyage,
for smoking, it smelled of the mud it was turning back into.
Age had brought it to that pass when its sex no longer counted,
nor the blotches on its skin, nor, barely, the flesh within,
coming apart like old rubber bands around old letters.

Eleven years ago my brother died and Heidi was a botanist
in Washington. Veronica, at eighty, was very much alive in Sussex;
James Taylor sang in Stockbridge. Why go back through it all?
To what spawn? "Carpe diem," the boss says, solving problems.

The sides of salmon stack like envelopes in brine. Tomorrow,
in the smoker, the dust of alder wood will burn beneath them.
Daphne will come the day after to pull a vacuum on the filets.
"You see where it glistens there," she'll say of her two. "That's
what I love. It's older than the dinosaurs, you know, the sturgeon is."

# THE SKINNING MACHINE

Over these memorial refrains,
like turtlenecks and Stevie Nicks,
the melody of "Suicide is Painless"
lilts, and the salmon-smoking process
reduces to a set of motions on repeat.

The quarterback keeps throwing a pass,
the linemen keep going for a sack.
Who pays attention to car alarms anymore?
Into a solution that doesn't flow,
into the brine they go,
the two sides to everything.

"Climbed a mountain and I turned around":
my brother used to mock that song,
but today, over the skinning machine
that slices too, neither he nor it is funny,
and the salmon, ready for high-end retail,
hold their shape on the golden board.

# A Favored Shape

The peach shapes a fan's exotic beak.
That hooks the mouth.
It's the *dorsum* in a fish
(humped up like a ginger cat
or a young girl rising from an early nap)
that hooks the spine—
a curve that holds in a medium blue Bic pen's cap,
and in the nose of my strange friend Peter,
like the tiny fish that join
the halves of a peanut together.
But the plum has a seam
where the peach has a fold
and the grape has neither.

## DE CHIRICO

Racks of selves
like garment centers
or targets out of Ariosto's shooting range.
Each allegorist phases things in
and phases things out.
Urinals, bric-a-brac, bananas, Zeus
cock at the looker,
the blancmange of the neck's stub.
*Cuori di carciofi*,
noon *urbi et orbi*,
the towering smokestacks,
dismembered eggs, girls with hoops
in angles of shade. He cleaned off storms,
restored cuts, buried fishes.
Mannequin, macadamia, *accademia*, harlequin
all in khaki, like an infantry.
His human scale
sloughed the weight of buildings off.

Heads of fashion, take note:
blanks adorn his runways,
heels click but no wood creaks,
gloves pin themselves to walls.

"I wish at any cost to be alone,"
he said. So the birds never came.
He staged his bald anatomies.
The only enigmas are fruit trees.

# THE CRAB

Which crustacean is it that goes
sideways and never forward?
Its is a habitable pattern, isn't it,
a mode of association?

Some need prodding to go on,
some to yawn before their debut;
all die, but few in a spineless sleep,
their identity saline, diffuse.

If it moved any slower, it would be hard to know
whether this creature could, like Prospero
or a big hitter in the major leagues,
be of good cheer, one thought out of three.

But since it somehow acknowledged proper
its going sideways, and goes, now,
sideways all the way, the crab has been
more cheerful than it would have been,

had it gone forward in the claw of another's wake,
and come up damaged on the farther shore.

# MOTIFS FOR A PORTRAIT OF TONY'S MOTHER

She wore white cotton most of the time,
flowers when she wore patterns,
and hats—wide-brimmed,
tawny straw hats, Panama hats;
had short blonde hair; was light,
very light; lots of yellow.

She must have been shy:
that must've been the read of her face,
a light lipstick, a silver;
not haunted, not innocent quite.
You would almost say frail,
but never sallow, never gaunt.

She had her own room
in the middle of the house
where she painted and read Wittgenstein.
We saw her only going in—except once,
when she came out and made us Ovaltine.

In going out to play, we saw what she'd
done with her brushes in the northern light,
easel holding the canvas to it;
some figures here, there none.

# FISHING

Trout sulk in a cool hole.
A yellow petal drops.
Our lenses polarize.
All ear, they rise,
their noses dimple-size.

We watch light change change,
shadows, swallows.
All flit, fit.
Fresh wings of the oldest sect
aren't hit.

The tied fly is.

Dave holds the fish he fought underwater.
He turns his head upstream
to flush its head of being caught.

Water takes us in its elementary eye.
A moose hears, lifts its head;
moss and water pour off
its mushroom-crooked rack.

# AFTER MY 20TH HIGH SCHOOL REUNION

## (1997)

The winding wind-fence shows the winding wind
how we think it ought to come in.

Two goats stand "where it's always safe and warm."
On a rise, five or six antelope face west.

The middle fork of the Crazy Woman meanders outside Kaycee.
"Mercy, mercy, mercy."

A dead cottonwood rests on its jaw
like a buck shot down.

"Sometimes, things don't lay as they're supposed to lay."
I'll start a licorice business.

# Buffalo Teeth

Hearts. Is nothing more to be said of them?
In their randomized, double-blind, placebo-controlled, stratified,
experimental design,
they look like buffalo teeth.

# DRIPPING FAUCET

The plumber took a look.
He couldn't stop it.
Choked flow.
Turn the knob, let it go.

You've got to go on.
Mom, poem—
what's the difference?

You've got to go on,
a knife-tip at the bottom of a jar
with no more peanut butter in it.

At the sink I wash
my dying face above
I hear my father say,
"Death is so common."

## II.

I often say to my foreign students: "I understand your sentence as a sentence, but I can't see what you want to convey. Was your sentence an assertion, a comment, an exclamation, a contradiction, a corroboration, or a question?"

—Harold Palmer, *English Intonation With Systematic Exercises* (1922)

# THE SOFT AND THE HARD

A cloistered molested tribe can't
democratize the solar system
liberally or conservatively.
The balance of costs, the soft
and the hard (i.e., all but the sun's)—
how can they be streamlined
and the Chinese not come out on top?

We're seeking new forms of finance,
—mutual, hedge, and pension—
the programmatic ones, not the penny-ante,
but the tax equity pool isn't big enough.
It's costing us already, which is how we know.
If we know anything, it's cost:
it's how we know anything exists.
But the softness of permission, inspection, connection—
we can't let these *fuwa fuwa* things get in the way
of a rapid-ass payback.

Still, there are neither hard not soft
but I would say shifting or loose
details that can cloud these projections.
They'll get costed in as we go.
And we'll look the toxins in the face.
They're out there; they're part of the process.
China just can't have them. We have to have some too.

Balance of system,
hard costs have gone down,
soft ones have gone up—
and what a revelation that was!
If I could just get my arms around this
I could paint a national picture.

# Lemon in Crinkly Paper

Pears, apricots, go away: screen more effectively
the sun from Emerson, articles on blackberry
bushes, my arms. I think I'm going to wait.

This meal, these undigested clouds, squat
building, fat lake, bitten apple at the hotel,
bowled, full of coffee and exhaustion,

a voice like that: roofed, derisive, apt.
Nothing but the best for the juiciest red
you can wear, chest or thigh, anatomy

intact—a Spanish impulse, sangria
Austin-style, fallen leaves like crickets'
shells. Jane has a question for you:

screened or screamed? Honest and good,
the end was, well, powerful—
which isn't a bad thing, in the event.

Heavenly, in fact, but not for the whole family.
The lake is a pig, in case you hadn't noticed,
full of iconography, inedible, smarter than hell.

There would be no novel, no epistle, no poem
without some handing down, the ur-*tractatrice*
gossiping at the salon. That's you:

let the bar graphs be rough and sketchy,
but don't think you can escape.
Milk always looks plentiful, being poured.

# Cognac and Milk

Greetings everyone, I hate you also.
A brilliant young fund manager quits her job
and ends her logarithm relationship
on a planet with more scientists than rainfall.
We see her begin to really think about
her job at the meat-penetration plant.
It's even more extreme than pundits thought.
And this is only in the last year,
just about eight minutes ago.

Milk-drinking may be a proxy for wealth.
Each new generation of cognac in any language
has a show called *Unremembered*
to pair with a show called *Unforgotten*.
Could you be spurred to flee your local currency in emerging markets?
It's work stuff.
The working stiff, God tried to keep the dollar in check.
Astronomers continue to play outside the Milky Way.
They clarify nothing triggering that could be concerning.
But who was the first person to ask, "Where are you going with this?"

# ON THE AFFINITY OF ALUMNI FOR TIME

On purpose, on form, on task, on point,
we wiggle from state to state.
One way to think about it is to say
fat thumbs on small keys often yield the sausage.
Is it time for touch yet?
Everyone asks that one, right?
It starts thinking about things you said—
*million*, *civilian*—and the crushing
realization drives the patient beyond
malice for therapy. "I know. I get it."
That's American conversation.
Long-form is a way of not saying *long*,
short-form of not saying *short*,
"as well" of not saying *too*.
Selfishness is still the main refrigerator.
Try not to get too abortional.
I want that interrogation excavated.
And then I want this excavation interrogated.
Don't "theorize" and then "give us your take."
How do you find an emotional arc in a zone loop?
I'm an incomer of not much.
My favorite dancer is the Khruangbin bassist.
Each of us sees over our own experience,
no matter how we feel in the sharp eyes of others.
I'm the world's only tautologist and justsostoryist
focused on the nontourism industry—
on the affinity of alumina for lime,
on the affinity of alumni for time.

# All

All western philosophy is a series of footnotes to Plato,
except Adam Smith.
All laws are defended or discovered with some heat, or both.
There are two kinds of human energy: *fact that* and *fancy that*.
Hackers are more effective than hecklers.
It's easier to cut an apple than an agate.
Instagram stores fears of losing its young users.
The dry bag is hogwash.
Is music reinventing sex all the time?
All famous people were once not famous at all.

# THE BEGINNING OF THE OCEANS

Leaves evolved to keep some raindrops from hitting the ground
at the same time as others. As the leaves got to be bigger,
and so able to hold up five or ten more raindrops,
they kept the sun from the smaller leaves, which died out.
The large leaves then began to flatten and form
what we know as lily pads, which eventually became
the surfaces of ponds and then of oceans,
where most of the raindrops that fell at different times
can now be found.

# Toccata

1.

The world's abrasive. Buildings are heavy.
But the earth is fairly firm.
The universe is tensile.

2.

We don't know what'll happen next.
The moment of contact is frightening.
We have affairs.

3.

There's no explaining the things people get good at,
or the people who get good at things,
or the things, or the good at.

4.

Need persimmons be orange
and oranges persimmon,
men men, women women?

5.

Sarah's living room was lofty and dark.
Then one afternoon she put on
The Allman Brothers Band, *Live at Fillmore East.*

6.

I lost the scarf my brother wove
from the coats of our neighbors' pets
and some of his own hair.

7.

But that was after I lost my brother.
At 88, I'll have consumed
300 tons of food and water.

8.

The word *shit* doesn't matter.
A family of four utters
21 pounds of it every weekend.

# What's My Problem?

We can jabber like a monkey in a tree, and we can rhyme ABAB.
"Donleavy, Mailer, Roth, Updike, some of the most important
men we have, are writing about cocks and cunts and arseholes
while I describe the summer dawn," John Cheever journaled.
I get inside my Aesthetic Fixation Bag
for a strangulationist interpretation,
the Initial Idealization: I'm 62.
The fact that Byron produced
800 double-columned pages of poetry
before he was lifeless at 36—
it's enough unidealization to make
his complete works alone a worthless chaos of study
more worthy than my time.
Global climate is overrated.
("Global climate is altered.")
What if we blacked the blue?
In the capital Concrete,
a moderate Islamist despot spoke to the people.
"I'm going on a little night shoot tonight,"
he said. "Ravaged by reading, I tire.
*Does* an ambulance of power invalidate sexual desire?
Was Heat Control not a respected Nazi ensemble
that mixed jazz and world music?" He started to mumble:
"*Palace* and *place*, like *cosmic* and *comic*, differ by a letter.
*Note* and *tone* differ by order of sounds. *Art* is *tar*."
He gripped the podium.
Back here, in an unlikely digital backwater, the facts are these:
  • we grew up in cheese together.
  • of the 100,000 automobiles in Argentina in 1924,
  73,000 were Fords.
  • the Monkees meant more to me than the Beatles.

Maybe that's my problem.

# III.

But whence (by the way) this odd generation of pleasure from pain? The movement of our melancholy passions is pleasant, when we ourselves are safe: We love to be at once, miserable, and unhurt.

—Edward Young, *Conjectures on Original Composition* (1759)

# Reading History in London (1979)

The secret of history appears to be
the devastation of names since the fourth century,
gold remaining remarkably steady.

There are many more important things
that I will say nothing about.
Even the surface of the sea is cruel.

Worship virgins, good manners, or both,
but either you love or you don't.
It's a great grace to be a woman:

more women are saved than men.
Barbarous Fritigern whispers,
"I am at peace with walls."

Words, words, and speech licks the night.
Unguent of song! Hash of noises!
O woods, O solitudes,

O Champagne, O Brittany,
who said that you were free?
So meager a ford, so crooked a road

the Saxons made from London to the sea.
"I am at best but a refined and affectionate cannibal,"
confessed the connoisseur, who stretched out

and divagated like unpainted clouds.
Scorta, meretrices, lupae stuck up at Vesuvius;
saffron, Paphian myrtle, amethyst;

pale rose, Thracian crane;
pepper on the trade routes, oil on the window panes.
The sun shined, it rained.

"No one can know which side's dead men
will win the war," wrote Janet Flanner,
and I sat there.

# THE FIFTH CRUSADE

Pope Innocent III, who thought man
but spit, piss, and dung,
who coined the phrase *persona ficta*
for Christendom,
sanctioned the pilgrimage to Palestine
after condemning Magna Carta.

The crusaders reached the Fertile Crescent
late in May, 1218. In August, Saint Francis
preached to them. They took Damietta
in November. They were in no hurry.
Five years passed.

They kept expecting
Frederick II, King of the Romans,
to come to their aid. He'd said he would;
he'd promised Innocent;
but he was busy with his astrologer.

When the Sultan ordered the sluice gates of the Nile
opened on the pilgrims, they'd had enough.
They were nostalgic.
When the Muslims attacked,
the Christians were drunk and confused.

They staggered into the bulrushes in the dark,
coughing on the smoke of tents and flesh and loot.
They stumbled into remnants of their ships
like pelicans, and sank; or they snored,
dreaming, as the infidels cut their throats.

Some say they were trapped by the river
and the devil; some, by their own emperor.
Others say they died for the plunder.
But then we know what it's like
not to want to leave the wine
in the land of those who don't drink it.

# Our Unsung Heroes

Our unsung heroes are better off unsung.
If you look at them in the latest book
concerning Lincoln's last twenty-four hours,
you see them scruffy, unkempt,
their dull black hair matted down.
They're all tied at the neck with those ties
Lincoln himself never cared to make appear tied.
Nicolay and Hay, his biographers,
look like they've already spent at least
another third of his life
writing that life—even as, his secretaries,
they're lean and hungry as Cassius.
None has a hairline full of hope:
not Speed or Colfax or Stanton
(his beard bigger than his head,
his eyes bigger than his spectacles)—
not Gideon Welles, who's narrowing down
the anecdotes of a presidential age.
William Seward's profile drowns
in a chinless, stiff-lipped sea.

Grant alone is groomed, but uncomfortable.
One of the sung, he doesn't know what to do
with his hands, now that the war's over.
One wants to rest in a deep pocket,
the other, to strip the uniform jacket.
Cross-eyed, pained, severe, Mrs. Grant
doesn't want the President to attend the theater,
and Mrs. Lincoln wears her black bonnet
like a winter of discontent.

Her husband knows that speech by heart.
He knows that summers are made glorious,
and thinks it doesn't matter how well or ill
Shakespeare is acted, "since with that writer
the thought suffices." And where thought's
concerned, he prefers in *Hamlet* the brother's
"O, my offense is rank, it smells to heaven"
to the stepson's more famous soliloquy.
"A comedy is best played; a tragedy
is best read at home," Lincoln wrote,
and never applauded with his hands,
though he always waited for the farce
that followed the main event, and laughed.

# PECKINPAH'S LAUGHTER

Four unimpartible things are:
faith, metaphor, the holding of liquor,
and whatever it is you're good at
just after someone tells you you are.

Off to what West are you heading?
Stay; the light is on the bush,
the scent of pine is flush.
Nothing but work lies ahead,
and nothing less behind—

but who are those guys?
Minor characters, bearing
sideways on storefront porches,
plus or minus a star
in the saloon, leaning on the bar.

In there, the liquor's amber,
the bottles have no labels,
the corks seldom stopper,
and Peckinpah's laughter,

actor for actor,
scores the killing.
Spun by gunshots,
they smash facades.

# To Squeeze Off

Two days ago I bought a newspaper for $1.3 billion in cash.
I read less than half of it. Then I tore off a third of Iraq and Syria.
After dinner I fell asleep. I was wasted.
Yesterday I got a tattoo and did some jihad.
I power-drilled a few skulls and blew up some shit.
I was amped. I put my father-in-law in a suicide vest.
Today they called me "a heavy drinker," "a thug and a pimp."
Explanation isn't popular. You've got to know what is.

History seems to be on failure's side,
trust on accident's, accident on planning's.
But some want to be seen to be acting.
They want that flower, safety,
plucked from this nettle, danger.
No fireman doesn't want a fire,
no goalkeeper not to be shot on.
Consider the sniper!
How arranged his danger,
how cocksure his safety.

# Representative Men

"Everything good is on the highway," Emerson wrote,
at his round desk in Concord, looking out on the route
to Boston, hurting for his prize pears falling early
and the poor woman screaming across the brook.

He wouldn't shoot the commuters with a rifle.
He'd say to him who would, "So hot, my little
sir, about your one objection?" then put a pear
in his pocket and take his daughter by the wrist.

They'd walk in the late afternoon,
no matter the weather, and work upon his heads—
Montaigne, Shakespeare, Swedenborg, Napoleon.
"What's the name of this river, Ellen?"

"The Onion, father." "*Oniona* it shall be, then."
"But you changed mother's name from Lydia to Lydian."
"To save my ears from neighbors saying *Lydier*.
I will not say Onion. How goes that novel by Grimm?"

"You're in it, father, as a character named Wilson."
"Wilson. Common enough. Good for him."
"Why don't you write about yourself, father?"
"*Ich kann nicht*—Onion! Strike Luther from my heads."

# The Rise and Spread

Removal is no remedy; posterity sees that.
With virtue go courage, liberty, and habit.
How could an oligarchy otherwise survive?
Brutus was passionate, intense, repressed—
a talker. A critic feels his shame for him
and ekes out his paltry part. Nothing's dubious
or irrelevant. It isn't necessary to believe the die
is cast, but all facets vanish when the cube discandies.
Then, a convenient wrong and a customary right
supervene. *Statio*, Augustus said, is only personal,
nothing business. Go on holding what you have
and get more: however remorseless the stability
of drift, whatever your desserts, however secure,
your *things done* are soon undone and outnumber
the items on your *agenda*. No grateful humanity
rushes to complete you. You too were authors:
uniqueness dissolves. Why notice "the new sect"?
They have time to commit a worse offense.

Feelings aren't the only things enlightenment
had a weakness for. Shall historians go on
distempered, appreciative, partial, insincere?
I didn't know reason had so many divisions.
Motives, desires, instincts, impulses, thoughts:
notwithstanding these retarded provocations,
studded with every fallacy you care to name—
*ad hominem*, intentional, *ad hoc*, even that of
misplaced concreteness—the resentful savior
remains a constant, touching but curious.
Equivocal birth, parents out of the picture,
travel, lecturing, men's groups, marketing—
yet deals were done and buy-in achieved.

56

Polished manners and a liberal education
had nothing to do with it. Gross fraud
issued in imperatives and anecdotes,
and no force rose to defend the group.

# A Note on Force

From William James, who got it from Alice Gibbens,
who got it from Kipling, who got it from Carlyle,
who got it from Thucydides:
civil order has for its ultimate sanction
nothing but force.
When you ask your neighbor to get his dog to stop barking
you see it of course.

# THE COURSE OF EMPIRE

Catholic-wise and back and forth
they go between rejections,
cursing their eternal promise,
drunk as Jesus, these Italians,
these poor Italians. They move
from *bella* this to *brutta* that—
*la musica, la gente*—
in this *inferno culturale*, America.

They come to be inside you, New York.
Turin's a grid, Milan's too German;
Rome was never good enough,
Venice drowns and stinks;
Florence is full of Americans.

Tired of being left behind,
*proprio qui* is a promise
they mean to keep: New York!
*Ma qui*, the crushed peppers—
*non sono buoni per fare*
*una puttanesca buona*,
and the oil's imported
(probably Spanish),
and the pasta's disgusting.

Independence loses its savor.
We know. And some horses
(remember Ethiopia)
will not be managed
after the laughing mode
of Castiglione.

But you were in Urbino then,
carving out the great future behind us;
now you come to claim
what our pure youth
took from Africa and Vespucci,
your imperial city-states,
your virgin Machiavelli.

# A TEXTBOOK CASE

The history editor pukes in the urinal
every day after lunch, then brushes his teeth
and hair. The tongue of his belt hangs out,
the sloven. He speaks at volume
but never at length, and saves his vacation
(sixty days and running) for the day when—

but all thinking is fuzzy, isn't it?
How clarity got to be a modern virtue,
why there are no degrees of uniqueness,
what word isn't equivocal.
Love isn't the main force,
and narrative won't fix it,
no matter how patiently and slowly
the thinker speaks, saying things often
depressing, boring, off the wall—

but "mail carrier" is better than "letter carrier,"
isn't it, and you come down in the end
against the semicolon, for continuity's sake.

# The Leisure of the Theory Class

There went Professor Veblen, the last man who knew everything—
the high gloss on a patent-leather shoe,
the same high gloss on a threadbare sleeve,
twenty-six languages.

He did his dishes with the hose.
He gave everything a C.

He went to his wife's house in the woods
with a black stocking in his hand.
When she answered the door, he said,
"Does this garment belong to you, Madam?"

# IV.

When I touch, I then begin
For to let Affection in.

    —Robert Herrick, "Love Dislikes Nothing"
(1648)

# WHAT STORIES ARE

You want to know what stories are?
You're quite a story yourself.
You're chronic and acute.

Say a man goes out with two rings on,
one on each middle finger,
does he like Morgan Freeman's voice?

My most masculine friend associated cigarette smoking with "sluts."
His mother never smoked, and he hated his mother.

I lay my place as my mother taught me to,
napkin left of the plate, fork on that napkin,
knife right, blade in, then spoon.

It's nice to be thought of.
It's even nicer to be told of being thought of.
I've taught English for thirty-five years.
I maintain a failure rate of ninety-five percent.

Language isn't a skill set.
It's the bone of contention.
But let's hear what you have to say.

# The Origin of Listening

Eve sanctioned touch.
Adam was too pleased with himself
to think about it much.

In Adam's pride,
men think writing and speech
lord it over grasp and reach.

In Eve's view,
God and Adam lied.
They never were or would be true.

They would always hide,
she had to infer,
and blame it on her.

# PATIENCE

I knew a girl who used to break boys in.
She had me kiss her on the forehead.
She felt like an old hand.

During a break from *Jesus Christ Superstar*
in the green room of our high school theater,
Chuck said she could get it to dance.

She touched this toy, this trifle,
and turned it into Patience, her theme.
"Slow down," she said. "Slowly. Slow."

She took me in hand. She showed me
that theater business, management of men,
was neither a dry run nor a pure thrill.

When her promise and my performance
were almost one, she looked me in the eye.
"My real name's Charlene."

## EMILY DICKINSON

Little hussy, loose morals,
said a woman who knew her.
She was crazy about men.

Passions are easily aroused,
but incomes are usually underreported
by about ten percent.

She terrified people without touching them.
Her great idea was breaking up.
You can't be immortal and live.

# Surgical Waiting Room

In a thumbed and fingered magazine,
life is motion. So says the advertorial.
Exceptions don't leap to mind. Station
comes and goes, and rock was molten.
A beautiful woman covers *Face* & *Wellness*.
Her photographer's credited. She's unnamed.
The red cockaded woodpecker may as well have one eye,
there are so many hand surgeons advertised.
Bison are staying in Chihuahua, *bison bison*,
but *homo sapiens sapiens* are migrating.
The things we make make us, says Jeep.

Now the Surgical Waiting Room is peopled.
I read about big black rhinoceros ears
and listen to human conversation.

     The body'll absorb that.
          I have my hearing aids out.
              I'm a little lost right now.
                   Nobody seems to like it. Why single me out?

Finger-pointing at big animals is considered bad form.
The surgeon comes for someone.

Rivers never look right in photographs.
The camera doesn't like them.
Three surgical stainless steel 420 screws won't fix that.

I touch the disinfectant dispenser
before I go in to hug my mother.
She says I'm a nice-looking man,
well put-together. Her dementia's advanced.

She's glad I don't have a love in my life,
because she wants "to be the one."

White noise can be moving.

"Your hair's tickling my face."
I pull my head away.
"I'm in great pain." I ask her where.
"Here, there, and everywhere."

We can't be sorry. We say we are and are.
Yesterday, as I opened the front door,
the neighbor across the street shoveling snow
fell over. I caused that by leaving my mother.

# To Finish the List

Where the birds sing without trees
to sing in, and jackhammers, pneumatic
mandibles, take up the slack, sinking in,
a rhythm section is forming. I pick up
without ease what they're putting down.
Asphalt and oil slicks have their poisonous
conversation; evergreens of annoying
tender-mindedness let every twosome
play through. Can I speak highly enough?
A squirrel lathes the skin off a tough nut.
My mother was always on the run, her eye
on her list. We had a funny romance
going on fifty years. To suffer in quiet,
never to complain, to finish the list
at last, is the height of manners.

## LETTERS

Of only one bundle could I say what my mother's old friend
said of one of her affairs: "The relationship came full circle."
("Whatever that means," my mother said.)

It took fifteen years for Sandra and me never to speak again.
The rubber bands around the other ten dry out and thin.
I'll have to replace them.

On Liz and Paula, on John and Bill, on Heidi's homemade envelope
and Veronica's *par avion* with its handsome trim; on Katie, Maro, Tim,
they stick without binding the sweetest phrase within: "I think of you."

Except on Jennifer's. "Fuck you," she closed, fifteen years ago.
But today, a card: "How's things?"
Then Love, a comma, her name.

# SINGLE BED

Liz preferred men older,
and one man to many,
but he was in Atlanta
and we were in Boulder.

She hung back at first,
like the figure
in the black cameo
she liked to wear.

Then all was fair:
every feature forward,
every surface glad
on the single bed,

the only kind
my mom let me use.

# A Note Left Behind (2003)

Today I came to see you,
feeling good about myself; stopped by.
Dressed in blue, of clear blue eye
I got from envy's power yesterday,
a girl of twenty's gaze, making coffees—
but you weren't at home. I was, away,
at home, for once, home to myself;
maybe you were too, away in your studio,
brushing paint. You don't like surprises,
right? Is it as we grow older, we grow less
surprised, less to want surprise?
You've forgotten my name sometimes,
when I haven't called, dropped by—
but I was clean and blue and fresh
today, or so I felt, and wanted you
to see me, see me, and give me
your hand, and lie with me.

# BARE ROOTS

When we hug sometimes as,
bare roots not being best,
freshly watered soil hugs
seedlings in their plugs,
no bell jar shivers,
no cell wall gives way.
When we need to be close,
"Hug me up" is what we say.

# IDEATED SENSATIONS

1.

In sweet peas as in France
sex determines chance.
Snapdragons lock their jaws,
poppies tear like paper.

Back in under cabinets dust builds
fascinated and trustworthy objects
disgusting to the touch. Fine mohair
piles at the base of refrigerator-freezers.

The sink drain catches waste.
The tub-ring holds all bathers.
Lust is moist and water runs.

2.

Should beauty be beyond words?
Champagne was never supposed to happen.
With the salty oil of mixed nuts
I groom my cocktail napkin.

3.

Raindrops pop on the roof
like floss from out between
a tooth and a tooth.

4.

The bumpy forehead of the goat,
the lithe body of the stoat,
the gerbil's nose, the cat's back,
the horse's throat.

Feel it push, the burr-head of the brother
you're holding under, the fly-ball in the web.
The violet, ivy, spear-head leaf,
the thing that's coming
under separate cover,
the kiss, the hug, the hand of the lover.

# ALL THE PRETTY MOTHS

Above the mud, where irrigation stalled in the bay,
in the miniature marsh, orange moths, moths of yellow
custard, old turquoise moths, ferrous green, tipped
and sought their balance like foals, or sod rolls
stacked crookedly on pallets just set down.
And the moon that bulks now at midnight so large
(what porch-light would be if it could be giant)
must have been making its way into this image
you called such a beautiful night and, lonesome,
took a walk along the back road in.

Just yesterday we were thirty, and ten the day before,
but the moon has never been fuller than it is tonight,
visceral, eviscerate with its sweet dream of light.
Insistent mother, enmeshed mother, beholding us
to discover why we need to talk so much, if not to her,
as if she couldn't suffice. Out of the skylight into the room,
sidereal traffic with its high beams, the light-industrial
district across the highway—nothing less than heavy retail,
densities incentivized to make our lives go a little better,
be happier somehow. The carpenters sleep; the killdeer
quit their peeping; the grass gains on the heavens
another fraction while we sleep, and all the pretty moths,
agreeing in the dark, stand on the standing water.

# Spearmint

The sprig of mint
that weeding grips
trips the mint
we medicined our juleps with
one May in Cherry Hills,
the horses at the gate.

Into blinders of cracked ice,
bourbon pours on from the fifth,
and when the green leaves
saddled with sugar
settle as the contents shift,
the horses break.

# Shoulders

Dancing alone in the middle of a motion
you know sometimes I will, catching myself,
smooth the boxer in me down and do you.
I'm in the tight corner by the door
when your shoulders take mine over,
when your head tugs mine right,
always right at first, then down
with a single pulse and forward
until I'm leaning with your weight,
dancing as though you were,
but a boxer still when your shoulders take mine over.

# V.

I do not strain at the position—
It is familiar—but at the author's drift

—Shakespeare, *Troilus and Cressida*, 3. 3. 112–13

# STALINIST

Stalin thought the Poles were good fighters,
especially when they fought against themselves.
I can be like Stalin in my thinking
and like the Poles in Stalin's thought.

# A Clear Name

We didn't wake up one morning having one, did we?
I've gotten up with someone else's on my lips—
Marx's, Mao's, Paul Newman's. We are one, no one,
and a hundred thousand, as Pirandello said,
and it doesn't matter at what point we are in our lives.

Sometimes the things I see in books are things I've heard
on the Senate floor, like the dualism of Gore and Specter.
And so I say to myself: books are facts, facts are like books,
the past has mapped my name, and I have to rally in it—
even though its roads are built for heroes to come to nothing in.

I look over my shoulder in the crisis and see the mountains unscroll.
It can't help but be distracting, like perfume at a funeral.
Then the series snaps. Subject to snapping myself and straying,
everywhere I look I have to keep looking. But what am I saying?
I'd rather climb in at a mouth than spy through the bone of a hare.

A man sneaks up on a trout in a stream that's perfectly clear.
Six foot five, he crawls toward the bank through the grass
so as not to cast his shadow on the surface ten feet tall.
In the event, the rainbow, not Dodge, is successful.
Race horses have more unusual names, but birthdays are fatal.

# THE NOOSPHERE

And what about the noctilucent clouds
that shower down on Gath
their daylong, ultraviolet bath?
They put us under dangerous rays
and make us suspicious of hot days.
We'll be praising snow and ice soon in new ways.
What about the longer, deeper, colder blue
we've after all been after?
This crust of mind our uplift grew
inhabits now no unhandselled savage veneer,
but a dog-eared, tattered troposphere
loaded like a die.

Still more this landfill wants
than its anatomy can conceal.
What sunblock for these cries
or toothpick parasol or shield?
The chlorofluorocarbons are not
subjects, objects, or verbs.
Their bond is on our skin
in rugged black dumbbells.

Is it, the noosphere,
with its indomitable aging lungs
and foot-dragging, the real article?
Or is it like the golf-green felt
stamped with chances on a table?
The toxic is our model.
And so is lyric piled on lyric
till the sun is met
with hothouse flowers and valid regret.

# Romanticism

Hothouse father, earth was first,
shoe-shaped as a Cornish pasty,
above us only sky.

These parking lots
we'll end up hating
level with us,

but you envy the Greek family
that collects on them,
the pagans,

from their shabby
little downtown outpost.
They do it effortlessly,

like contortionists,
which is what rubs you raw,
perfectionist.

You taught me nothing but
Kipling's wanderlust
and Camus' rebellion

against his own revolt.
Romanticism, you said,
means looking back.

I am, can't not—
and there you are,
telling me to honor you.

# In Praise of Older Men

I like the wise, serene company
of older men. Most of my life's been
spent with them—their validation,
their acceptance, their tortures

of forgetfulness, the massive
irritation of what they know.
The complications, too; I like
the accompaniment of older men,

men a little older than my father,
men a little younger than my father;
men nothing like my father,
men my father wouldn't like.

I like their reassurance, the cooking
and what can only be described as
the *rawing* disbelief they can express:
it borders on the abject,

if such a standard exists. "God,"
my father thought in reading me,
"I hope he didn't plagiarize this."
But there's a little larceny in every heart.

## Keep Your Shoulders Back

My father liked handsome men.
He showed me how to notice them.
"He carries himself like a boxer, that man.
I bet he used to fight." (In church, he ushered.)

He'd sometimes say, as I was going out at night,
"Don't be in a hurry to get married, and don't
be afraid to marry a rich girl." Once, surprised
at himself, he said with admiration and contempt:

"You have more moves than a belly dancer,"
and kissed me on the lips goodbye. Then:
"Keep your shoulders back and your chin up,
and keep your mouth closed when you breathe."

# IN THE STRAWBERRY FIELD

Doctor J walks the field with Stash and me and Gene, a geneticist
from the USDA, scouting the runners' three-leaf clusters for the berries
they hide. They find a good one, because firm and, they believe without
checking, red clear through—then chuck it and pick another, just as good,
and throw it to the ground. The next one Gene picks I put out my hand for
and get. They pass on, reviewing their creations. In the end, they want
only firsts in every category, one of which is field-life. Pomologists,
the doctor says, live long lives. "This is in history." He's fourteen years
into his search for the perfect berry. He says we can feed our brains
on his fruit. I tell him the doves must. "Yes, the doves. And the deer.
They give us lots of trouble."


The berries show in their plants like LEDs, red as scrapes on your knees,
redder than the big bright Texaco star used to be. They purple where
the doves peck them into jam, and you can see the centripetal tail
of each epidermal seed streak to stoneless center. Stash and I pick
what the doctor's flagged for color, size, and flavor. We find the whitish
all through sweeter than the solid red. From underneath, the patch is fall:
clipboard browns, school-bus yellows, Ked oranges ripen in leaves
over so much fruit abreast the berries bruise themselves and leak in the press.
In the furrow, I mistake lambsquarters for clover and shreds of plastic—
last spring's choke on pineapple weed and purslane—for arrowheads.
Stash pockets coins, glass, clay pipe stems. Watching from the last field
of winter rye, a woman opens sandwich bags of transplants from the lab.
She calls over, "Don't knock yourselves out weeding. No shelf-life in those.
Doctor J's having that field plowed under." But we're eating, not weeding,
and we go and show her.

# BUDAPEST, JANUARY 15, 1983

It's an irony city, surfaces unreflecting little mustaches in the sky.
Sky should be thrown out of this craft, this chaotic guild.
Out of paprika sauces last night we ate cabbage
and the taste-budded guts of ox, Magyarest cabernet
from a beer pitcher, red plates and waxen yellow napkins.
Like a cat's tongue on your fingertip against your tongue.
And slashed ribbons of stomach tissue translucent brown,
unlike the river—or that attaching piece of skin
under your tongue: I tasted it in my idea of what I was eating.
The paprika somewhat covered for it, and the slivovitz
peasants had made. Peasants! the poet said in English.
Three vapor punches of it each before the meal,
off the roof of your mouth like a doctor's office,
the plums lurking behind like nursery rhymes
but splitting your lips' skin. I threw up twice that night.


                              in memory of István Eörsi

# Editorial Assistant

Office air in the afternoon,
the post-lunch dip,
most phones still forwarded.
A fan shakes in its boot
on a cubicle ledge.
Manila folders, a small coffee.
"Haydn invented classical music."
"All assistants are subject to change."

# TYPE

Its biggest self,
a cicada drops dead
a perfect specimen—
dry, intact, relaxed.

# VI.

O, my friend, let us labor onwards
in the narrow path! Even in far Colorado
there must be tasks for the pious soul to do.

—F. W. H. Myers to William James (1895)

# In Far Colorado

Illumination of it came from London,
in a room I didn't understand,
boy-sized, but bigger than a coffin.
The wallpaper had roan stallions
flanked by cowboys and Indians,
all grounded on a big blue sky.
I lay on the bed like a shovel,
either hand in spitting distance
of a pint of White Horse and a puck of Skoal—
part of the cartoon. But the cloud
drawn over me shed the jobless moans
of a Belfast couple and the stale taunt
of a bloke at Bentham's godless college:
"Oversexed and over here." I was far
from an authentic Allied souvenir,
and liked it better when he called me,
a blonde with manners, "swarthy and rude."
It was the Day of the Dead, All Souls,
when I moved; the Plantagenet roses hung
like grapefruits by the stoop.
I could hear hymns from the church, sung
through my longing and my pity and my hurt.
So I went back on these, an ocean
and a Kansas of highways yet from home,
by what seemed to me then the only way.
I went back to my corner in far Colorado
and wrote down the terms of my stay.

# FAMILY

Families aren't like salmon filets,
though they too seem to grow
from the inside out—
and don't resolve in lines
from a single spine; have no pin-
bones a pair of pliers can remove;
can't be decided at the neck—
which, as Hitchcock would note,
is the perfect cure for a sore throat.
One can say, "Drive carefully"—
and never mean, in a family,
"I hope you get in an accident."
The heart of it is a broken heart,
and sciences younger than ichthyology
have failed it.

# Starting to Quit

Spoiled and addicted, I couldn't take my father's wisdom
when he gave it, that the only way to quit is never to start.
I was off in his footsteps and off in my mother's, who was
off in hers, the cocktails and cigarettes by then pretty well
*per stirpes*, as lawyers say in wills. Drinking and smoking
went hand in hand, as the profiles of Wystan make Auden.
I got drunk first at a brunch for the resurrection.
The champagne rushed down the flutes and rose again.
We drank according to the scriptures, my father and I,
keeping always in the back of our minds the verse
that everyone remembers their last martini
but no one remembers their first.
Who was counting?
We didn't check our thirst,
the cups it took to get us to recite
the old poems of the inner life,
its melancholy, choked-up light
that brimmed with all the craft or sober art
we often envied in the poet
and sometimes hated.

# DEVILED HIGHWAY

Love's labor's not always lost.
I grew in a suburb and saw.
After storms there was wonder,
there was loving and reconstruction.
I was born in one, and I'm still
dragging branches to the field
and raking up my twigs.
The same went for my parents.
They had feelings too.
They would have liked to move
to another neighborhood,
but they stayed. In the room
where one of us died our mother
kept her office as before.
She was an interior decorator.
On the corner where one of us
was killed, our father still
cut and swept and trimmed.

My brothers and I committed
crimes, did drugs, had sex.
We lied, we cheated, we hid.
We were in our father's eyes
milestones to American liberty.
Until 1967, he marched us
mornings with the flag
to the window facing west,
unfurled it, saluted, put it
like a soldier in its post,
made sure our hands
were on our hearts,
then led us in the Pledge.

In our mother's, we were
apostles of the Catholic faith,
god-mothered, god-fathered,
innocent, best in navy blue
with knee socks and saddle shoes.

Division was always imminent.
Every day on the way to school
the "Divided Highway" sign
read "Deviled" to me,
and many divisions since then
have come to pass.

# AT FAIRMOUNT CEMETERY

Each of us holds something:
purse, Bible, whiskbroom,
hairpin, gloves, flowers, keys,
hand. Picks at something—
grass, dirt, trash.
We start saying things.
We look at the crabapple trees
if it's that time; if not,
at the mountains through their branches.
We look out, up, away
from the leanings the headstones
have, but end up looking down
at the four of us we came for.
Then we read from scripture.
That makes us weak.
The "Our Father" makes us weaker.
We want to hurry up and go.
Our hips face the headstones,
but our shoulders cheat to the car.
That's the kind of animal we are.

## Deathbed, beginning with lines from

## Felicia Hemans

*O call my brother back to me,*
*I cannot play alone.*
*The summer comes with flower and bee—*
*Where is my brother gone?*

The day he died was warm and dry;
dust was on the lawn.
December snow was pushed back high
near rails no train rolled on.

"He isn't there," my father said,
"Come on with us outside."
Then took my hand to pull my head
from the cold tide.

"He isn't there," my father said,
and grabbed me by the arm—
then let it fall and left the bed.
A breeze came in and broke the charm.

# Elegy for Craig (1984)

Craig is on top of a ship crossing the Irish Sea
toward Ireland. He has never been there.
Around him is a greatcoat, around him like a wheel.
Around his neck he wears the scarf he made of hairs he spun.
He is lying on his back looking up at all the truths there are.
He believes they are as many as the stars.
He makes out faces in the constellations, faces all his own.
With his magic hand Craig traces lines to link,
ways to distinguish them.
To the Irishmen going home for Christmas he tells
ten jokes in a row, and has them rolling.
Now he includes them in all the little things he knows,
the things he found where three roads meet,
and then he lets them go.
He brings together the folds of his clothes
like waves in his fingers, feeling them goodbye.
They are all he has left of the musculature of the mountains
he loved lifting up into the sky. In his mind he goes
the motions of a camera, a loom, a press, a screen,
a clean white sheet of the best rag.
His fingers sing on the black keys—
"No place ever seemed like home to me."

I hope it wasn't always that you were riding high and fast
when I was low, and you were down and blue
when nothing could've been better for me.
But we were always proud of how well our wishes went,
and knew as well the sorrows as the majesties
of being independent. Craig, so smooth, so perfect,
so loving to go from the turn into the sprint.
It will take such a long time for us
to catch up with you, you went so fast, but we will.

# DEATH

Don't mouths stay open at the end?
Aren't lips parted?
They always close the eyes
with a soft sweep of palm.
If the mouth were open,
the palm would carry on
to join the lips,
but it never does.

## In Bed

I stay awake, needing to sleep,
to hear the song I want to fall asleep to,
which I want to hear as I sleep
and stay awake to listen to.

When death comes, I hope it will come
like sleep at night, when I'm reading in bed,
and I'll want to keep reading, and turn off the light, and go to sleep
all at once.

# VII.

A smooth, closely shaven surface of grass is by far the most essential element of beauty on the grounds of a suburban home.

—Frank J. Scott, *The Art of Beautifying Suburban Home Grounds of Small Extent* (1870)

## After the Storm

Mrs. Colburn called the beauty terrible, and Mrs. Boucher agreed.
Some of the limbs could have wrecked a car or killed someone.
My mother said it was one of those nights when you heard
breaking off all around, and my father said there hadn't been a night
as bad for trees since the night of the storm I was born in.
"Looks like a war's been through here," Mrs. Colburn said,
waving and on her way. Nothing to do then but drag the dead
across the snow and throw them on the pile. We'd had our say.

# LANDSCAPE AND SPRINKLER

Woody to get us going says,
take it to the bigass,
put the screws to it,
put the whoops to it,
put the fucks to it,
but don't kink the piss out of it.

I see what he means,
since we work with water and we work in dirt.
He says when I've taken down a trench,
take it down another hair,
and I see what he means
different from before.

Nobody goes six feet deep
unless it's for effect.
We go that far and farther
to find the main that feeds the house water,
then tap it and turn it to our purpose.

When the sun goes down,
our bucket heads like soda guns
confuse the juniper with gin.
We stand and watch our nozzles
light the lawn with rainbows,
the new wisteria with mists.

Woody to get us going says,
put the shovels in the truck.

# Putting in the System

I chop the cricket's thigh.
The beetle's amber back
breaks when the shovel insists.
I mangle bluegrass.
Sod splits in my ear
like a segment
from a segment of orange.
Trenches lengthen, deepen, veer.
The sun stiffens a track of dirt;
worms strung along it
burn like hair.
Cumin rises in the air
on vapors from the glue
that binds together there
male valve ends
and female pipe.
I dig the housing down
to seat the valve box
a thumb above
the level ground,
then shovel backfill
back in up around
until the system's hole's
a surface
sod will hem in.

# LAYING SOD

Sod's almost more alive when delivered and scrapped
than when laid. It comes stacked on the flatbed like shade
in six-foot rolls, which is what they're called in the trade,
though I'd rather call them slabs. You stagger them
when you undo them on the earth, the second one
cut roughly in half, the third whole, like the first,
and so on, until you have a lawn. If you get off track,
you can fix a sod-line the way you heal an injured
sweater, by jiggling the stitches until they give you back
in the disappearing snag the pleasure of the mesh.
In a month it will all be one, and you won't really see
the stabbing and the hacking and the slitting
with the sod-knife there had to be, to get it to butt up,
contour, and conform. The scraps that come of that
make like snakes when you fling them into the trailer,
slinking down when they strike the heap and molding
by contraction to it. I want to save the good pieces—
the tails, pelts, and hides—even though I have no place
in mind for them, no prospect of another job I might
use them in for salvaging spots the sun's burned out,
or patching berms a mower couldn't help but scalp.
But the whole idea of the lawn is phasing out,
and I'm laying more rock than sod.

# CALLBACKS

I'm not sure how it all worked,
but we pushed the black poly pipe
onto the male parts—l's, t's, and 90's—
crimped it to the bigass, then buried it
up to where the heads had to be screwed on,
so that if any dirt got into the system
(and it always did) we could flush it out
before we went ahead and set the nozzles.
"Bury it," the boss always said, "Bury it."

So we filled back in what we dug out
(and it was always more than we dig out),
turned the cut-out sod right-side-up again,
then stomped it down along the trenches.
It almost looked like nothing had happened
when we left, and everyone was happy.
But the dirt wouldn't stand for it.

Two weeks later, the people called to tell us
there were depressions in their lawn deep enough
to sprain their children's ankles. The blueprint
didn't call for swales, and the sprinklers
needed adjusting: they were supposed to cover
the lawn, the shrubs, the beds, and the new trees—
not the porch when they had guests over
for cocktails and hors d'oeuvres.

So everything we went and fucked up once
we had to go back and fuck up again.


for Bruce

119

# Nice House

Sprinklers work opposite the rain and make themselves ridiculous,
but no one's home to turn them off. The lights, too, waste away
in the living room, where a black terrier keeps a yellow tennis ball in play.
When the people come home, they let the dog out, turn the sprinklers off,
let the dog back in. They tell each other they're tired, turn the lights off,
turn in. The dog alone persists. His ball's the bright spot in the house,
his lawn's the greenest on the block, and all his systems go.

## SAMANTHA

She crossed her paws.
She always tried the new snow
with the real black of her nose.
She made me want to do that.

She was a little lion.
They said she was a cross
between a Norwegian elkhound
and a poodle, and sold her for three dollars.

Sam was what I am,
except she was never trained.
"Come here, good dogger, come on,"
I'd say in my nicest voice;

and when she'd come,
"Bad dog, go on, get outta here."
She did both. I think she had a choice.
Good dog, bad dog.

Whatever moral sense I have
when I use and don't use those words,
I owe some of it to hers.
She was a good dog, Sam, good dog.

for Lizzie

# REFRAIN

The circular saw cuts through it.
No dream, no speakers, can bear it.
Skilled labor doesn't care.

Framers tilt back their cans of beer
and ignore the refrain:
"I'll stop the world and melt with you."

But I've lived too long in a kind of school,
if it's possible to live too long in a kind of school,
to ignore the refrain,

and it's Saturday, and everyone's working.
Sunbathers have begun to double-park
and smear themselves against the sun.

My dream is in ruins, but I'm not,
and I happen to like this song,
especially the refrain; so I'll sing along.

# VIII.

yet felt, from time to time,
The littleness that clings to what is human

—Henry Irving, *Isaac Comnenus, A Play* (1827)

## STILL LIFE

The plums get heavy
in themselves.
They weigh the table down.
Bananas leopard
and Formica disappears.
The last peach gets antsy
at its bruise.
Spores form in teal.
The summer-blue stems
whose tags are on them still
catch dust in their bulbs.
The gas station bonus glass
touches the loving cup
and the recipes cut from the news.
The pantry has two cans.

# COOKING ON CAMERA

The chopping of the chocolate, the zesting of the orange,
the scalding of the milk, the pouring of the cream,
the folding-in, the stirring-of, the spoon against the glass,
the knife on the cutting board: we hear it all
as intimately as our own mastication
and deglutition, our kissing and coition.

But where's the *ur*-starter, the *echt*-roux?
Where are the prep cooks, the fuss in the pantry,
the picking and the packing, the trucking and the pricing,
the lifting and the stashing, the seeding and the skinning,
the peeling and the mashing?

Here, chopped is mixed and mixed is baked and baked is finished.
It's a paradise of latent content, in which the meal above board
has a stand-in off-camera, and the table's set for life.

But the paucity of our kitchens! The sordidness! The disorder!
Where are our tongs? Our eighteen pans? Our wonderful knives?
Our one-of-each-of-everything laid out
with a duplicate of each in easy reach?

Time, that ultimate sauce, reduced almost to nothing,
then supplemented with overlap, plenitude, and repetition;
things done that can't be repeated,
tips in profusion, hints, techniques, advice, butter;
a towel always on hand and handle,
nothing spilled, no slips between cup and lip,
only renderings, clarifications, infusions, dissolves;

processes with the process removed,
without the baking time being taken;
that accomplished dish without accomplishment—
that insouciance and measure,
those nested sets of Pyrex cups,
the stainless patter, the perfect batter,
the crude, the cooked, done to a turn, and nothing burned;
the egg festooned, the icing squozen,
the raspberry drizzled, the potato stuck, the capers
in the rustic mayonnaise snuck, and no dishes to do:
fucking cooking.

# ACTION MOVIE

Let's do this.
(87 minutes later)
You good?
I'm good.
We're done here.

# THE GENESIS OF TALLULAH BANKHEAD

She said, "Come with me.
This is the house, this is the way."
We got down on our hands and knees.
She was very small, 14 by 15, so I said
I couldn't follow her because I was 33.
She said I was foolish, that half that is around 16.
I told her I was afraid of small places,
but she took me into them.
In these rooms, there were pictures of her,
Tallulah, her hair in ringlets,
a headband of black silk.
"I used to do this," she said, "and that."

# GINGERLY

How gingerly we must in our way
be absolute, yet never come to say
the thing we came to say.

We don't know better and we're going to die.
But that's not what's the matter.
I wish I were again what I was once,
a clean wipe, good for one clean swipe,
but time won't let me.
A Buddhist can be a dentist.
A mechanical pencil can have no eraser.

Learning takes time—
except when it hardly takes any,
if learning's even what's taking place.
A mistake's a mistake.
But that's a mistake.
An eraser erasing is erased.

# ANGER

Why do you always have to start crying just after I start?
You always have to ruin it for me.
Why can't you bear it without taking part
when the grief is not your grief
and the heart is not your heart?

# Training Up in Calendar Software

How can we get caught up in the past,
where no one's available?

Other questions?
No, it doesn't matter how we shadow our twilight hours.

As the calendar fills, we chug away in the background.
Questions while we do?

Can we do it any faster?
Everything goes away eventually, but the process can't be hurried.

Privacy? Artifacts of others' calendars will always be in yours.
You can only hide yourself.

# A LIFE

Disposed to like it when I began,
I found it in the end an also-ran.
For being so long, it's far too bitty.
Inside every good book is a shitty.

# THEORY OF MIND

Most of the time
I'm aware
I'm depressed
I'm okay
I'm depressed
I'm aware
I'm okay
most of the time.

# LAST-MINUTE SHOPPERS

As when we went to the cemetery, all hands are full.
The wind whips it up, the pretty lanterns light it up.

Some of us have waited this long to do the right thing,
escaped from freedom many times to be strangled by skyline

that pitches on the Hudson lights from an even-handed city.
It isn't a question of time management.

Jersey-side, where portions are large
and on occasion you can see a clean white limo

stretch along,
buildings hang like stockings from the water.

# ACKNOWLEDGEMENTS

Some of the poems in this collection appeared originally in the following publications:

*ÁCOMA, Rivista Internazionale di Studi Americani*
The Course of Empire, Our Unsung Heroes
(as Lincoln and Shakespeare)

*Dionysos: Journal of Literature and Addiction*
Starting to Quit

*The Noe Valley Voice*
Nice House (as Superfluity)

*The Paris Review*
Cooking on Camera

*Raritan: A Quarterly Review*
Peckinpah's Laughter

*Studies in American Culture*
A Note on Force (as A Note of Force)

*The Wallace Stevens Journal*
The Noosphere (as Our Regret)

# ABOUT THE AUTHOR

Mark Scott was born in 1959 in Denver, Colorado. He was educated at the University of Colorado, University College London, Università per Stranieri di Perugia, and received an English Ph.D. from Rutgers, The State University of New Jersey in 1992. Mark is currently living in Japan, where he is Professor of English at Nara Women's University. He has been nominated for the Pushcart Prize and won the Academy of American Poets Prize in 1992. His work has appeared in numerous print and online publications, including *Poetry*, *Santa Monica Review*, *The Kenyon Review*, *Western Humanities Review*, and *Streams of William James*. His two previous poetry collections are *Tactile Values* (New Issues, 2000) and *A Bedroom Occupation: Love Elegies* (Lumen Books, 2007).

# ABOUT KINGSTON UNIVERSITY PRESS

Kingston University Press has been publishing high-quality commercial and academic titles for nearly fifteen years. Our list has always reflected the diverse nature of the student and academic bodies at the university in ways that are designed to impact on debate, to hear new voices, to generate mutual understanding and to complement the values to which the university is committed.

Since 2017 all the books we have published have been produced by students on the MA Publishing and BA Publishing courses, bringing to life a range of community and creative projects, often partnering with organisations from our local community or poets from the university's vibrant writing community. While keeping true to our original mission, and maintaining our wide-ranging backlist titles, our most recent publishing focuses on bringing to the fore voices that reflect and appeal to our community at the university as well as the wider reading community of readers and writers in Kingston, the UK and beyond.

@KU_press

www.ingramcontent.com/pod-product-compliance
Lightning Source LLC
Chambersburg PA
CBHW050900180626
46814CB00007B/2815